Hiking Trails
&
Gospel Truths

Hiking Boots
&
Gospel Truths:

Building Testimonies
in the Outdoors

MARK D. HARRISON

CFI
Springville, Utah

This is not an official publication of The Church of Jesus Christ of Latter-day Saints. The opinions and views expressed herein belong solely to the author and do not necessarily represent the opinions or views of Cedar Fort, Inc. Permission for the use of sources, graphics, and photos is also solely the responsibility of the author.

ISBN 13: 978-1-59955-282-8

Published by CFI, an imprint of Cedar Fort, Inc., 2373 W. 700 S., Springville, UT 84663
Distributed by Cedar Fort, Inc., www.cedarfort.com

Library of Congress Cataloging-in-Publication Data

Harrison, Mark, 1950-
  Hiking boots and gospel truths : building testimonies in the outdoors / Mark Harrison.
    p. cm.
  ISBN 978-1-59955-282-8
  1. Nature--Religious aspects--Church of Jesus Christ of Latter-day Saints.
  2. Witness bearing (Christianity)--Church of Jesus Christ of Latter-day
Saints. 3. Spiritual life--Church of Jesus Christ of Latter-day Saints. I.
Title.

  BX8643.T45H37 2009
  261.8'8--dc22
                        2009010933

Cover design by Jen Boss
Cover design © 2009 by Lyle Mortimer
Edited and typeset by Heidi Doxey

Printed in the United States of America

10 9 8 7 6 5 4 3 2 1

Printed on acid-free paper

To my wife, Debbie, who held down the fort while I headed off
into the wilderness year after year, gathering the experience
and material to write this book.

Contents

Preface:
Why the Wilderness

I grew up in the Northwest, by Mt. Rainier. In scouts and with my family I camped and hiked throughout the ruggedly beautiful Cascade Mountains. Each outing was a pronounced adventure for me, but each adventure also subtly infused in me something intangible, unnoticed at the time, but deeply affecting, a connection with a heartbeat found in nature— nature's spiritual side.

I was seventeen when I initially became aware of the wilderness's spiritual aspects. One night while I was camping with some friends at Mystic Lake below Mt. Rainier, I awoke in the middle of the night thinking it was morning because of the brightness inside the tent. I climbed out of my sleeping bag and stepped out of the tent, but instead of the sun greeting me, I beheld a full moon radiating through a clear sky, reflecting off the snow-covered sides of Mt. Rainier onto the bare slopes of the mountain immediately across the lake from me. It was like a spotlight shining off a mirror. I almost had to shield my eyes. I wasn't sure whether I was dreaming or not. But the scene didn't go away, and I stood there uncomprehending and dazed. Despite my being mesmerized, something inside me caused me to realize that I was seeing God at work, and I thanked Him for allowing me to glimpse the power of His artistry.

Fifteen years later, another similar moment occurred when I was taking a group of older youth to Mt. Rainier. As we drove through the valleys and canyons on the east side of the mountain, we listened to classical music to complement the vistas around us. I played *Die Mouldau* by Smetana, a piece which grows with inspiring crescendos. Just as the music came to a particular climax we, by some providential coincidence, also reached the top of a ridge, and with no hint or transition, Mt. Rainier burst before us in larger-than-life reality. It caught the young men by surprise, and they quietly stared at the beauty and grandeur of the sight. After a while, one turned and said, "Thank you for bringing us here." Not immediately, but later when I had a chance to ponder that young person's comment, I wondered what it was that made him respond with such reverence and appreciation. I began to realize that when in the presence of some grandeur in nature, a force causes us to kneel spiritually and to acknowledge an immense, humbling power, similar to what King David felt when he exclaimed in Psalm 8:3–4: "When I consider thy heavens, the work of thy fingers, the moon and the stars, which thou has ordained; What is man, that thou art mindful of him? And the son of man, that thou visitest him?"

I harbored these ponderings, thinking they were thoughts particular to my life experience until one day when I was talking with a friend. He was describing a long-distance hike he had recently finished in the Cascade Mountains of Washington State. He described a particular event along a trail. He and his group had rounded a bend in the trail where the trees parted, allowing a magnificent view of giant granite peaks covered with evergreen forests and rushing streams so seemingly close that it felt like he could reach out and touch them. My friend and the other adult with him paused. Something welled up inside of them, and spontaneously both began singing "How Great Thou Art." I knew that trail. I had hiked that very section, and I knew why they started singing that hymn. I wished I had known that hymn at the time I had been there so that I too could have expressed my praise and appreciation more completely.

With that conversation, I began to understand why being out in nature was so important to me. I realized that being in the wilderness is a great tool by which the Lord can help us as parents or youth leaders to grow and develop young people's relationship with their Heavenly Father. I had always had prayers with the youth on campouts, mainly to petition for safety and to bless the food (with good reason), but now those prayers while kneeling around the campfire seemed to have more emphasis on the experience in the wilderness environment as well. I began to find meaning and spiritual insights in most of what the young women and young men and I did, and not because I brought any inherent capacity to the opportunities, but because the spiritual meaningfulness was inherent to the environment and the activity in it. All we had to do was go and participate.

Initially, I had gone on these excursions just to try to help the youth have a good experience, but as frequently became the case, I and they came away far more helped and blessed from our wilderness adventures than by just having a good experience. What follows are accounts of some of the more meaningful stories, along with the associated spiritual insights gained, that I experienced while serving youth or my own family in the wilderness. I earnestly hope these experiences will help the reader find interest in using the wilderness as a resource for teaching gospel truths and learning from the Spirit.

Introduction

Most of us from our early years have enjoyed vacations, picnics, and family outings to the mountains, lakes, or parks. I would wager, with few exceptions, that most have fond memories of having fun with family and friends out in nature. Those memories, in and of themselves, probably merit the efforts it took to make the events happen. The bonding alone confirms the beauty and need of those outdoor experiences. Something about being out in God's domain refreshes. But after having spent years going out to nature with youth groups, family, and just by myself, I have come to realize that the wilderness can do more than just refresh. The wilderness can aid in teaching gospel truths and providing spiritual insights in unique and powerful ways.

As parents or youth leaders, we constantly seek ways to make events meaningful and spiritually beneficial for our youth. As youth leaders, we strive to find a purpose for activities: Young Men leaders seek to involve the purposes of the Aaronic Priesthood; Young Women leaders seek to involve the values of the Young Women's theme. As parents, we strive to teach gospel truths and provide opportunities for our children's testimonies to grow. There are a variety of scenarios and occasions available to accomplish these goals, but I have found that the wilderness offers one of the more unique and powerful channels by which to do so. From nearly two hundred youth and family outings, I have collected a variety of wilderness guidelines that can help give family or youth group outings greater meaning and spiritual benefit.

The chapters in this book have been organized to feature a guideline, an insight, and a story relating how the wilderness can be a resource for learning gospel truths and gaining spiritual insights.

The Guideline

The guideline is a general statement that youth leaders or parents can adopt or adapt to their particular needs and geographic environment. Guidelines are stated as principles such as "Activities that take us out of our comfort zone make us good students" or recommendations such as "Use wilderness activities to serve as gospel object lessons." The guidelines mentioned in this book are not meant to be seen as the sum total of all possible guidelines but as the ones which were most meaningful to me.

The Insight

Each guideline has an accompanying spiritual insight attached to it that illustrates a principle or truth that may be derived or expected from following a particular guideline.

The Story

Each story is about a specific wilderness event that helped me to see the insight and develop the guideline. It is the story that brings the guideline to life and serves as a catalyst for the reader's adaptation and imagination. The stories reflect learning situations taken from Young Men, Young Women, and family outings. No matter which group the story is about, the respective guideline and insight can certainly be adapted to either Young Men, Young Women, or family activities.

Although the insights and truths mentioned here were ones that I most clearly perceived, a particular guideline may lend itself to serving as a catalyst to a variety of meaningful spiritual lessons and emphases. The important thing to remember is that wilderness activities are a much more significant source for revealing and teaching gospel insights and truths than we may initially give them credit for. The secret is getting out into nature, getting out frequently, going with a guideline, and praying that the Lord will bless the wilderness activity to be the great spiritual resource that it can be.

1

Challenging Activities

Guideline: Challenging activities can provide opportunities to serve and care for others.

Insight: I am my own best keeper when I am my brother's keeper.

The Mountain

We left at midnight. The glaciers and snowfields were more stable in the cold of the night—less chance of an avalanche or snow bridge breaking. We were six older teenage boys and two adults intermixed in a climbing party of twenty-five, all with the single objective of making a successful ascent to the summit of 14,410-foot Mt. Rainier.

For the better part of a year, our Explorer group had been training and preparing, conditioning ourselves for what is known as the hardest climb in the "lower forty-eight." We had run up and down sand hills with rocks in our packs, walked with weights on our ankles, ridden bicycles up steep hills time after time, and hiked cross-country straight up our local mountain peaks. We had spent time training with our guides in rope techniques and ice axe handling. And now here we were, standing at the edge of Cowlitz Glacier, roped together in our five-man ascent teams ready to take our first step onto the ice.

I noticed that the boys were uncharacteristically quiet, probably for the same reasons I was. We were all mentally reviewing equipment lists, inwardly fearing we hadn't trained hard enough, and maybe just praying that sometime the next morning we would all be safely atop the formidable mass of snow, rock, and ice looming above us.

For the tenth time I adjusted my headlamp, making sure its light shone down at just the right angle. I was the last man in the last rope team. The other four teams had already departed and were stretched out in front of me like a long strand of Christmas lights. Occasionally a headlamp would bob, and I could guess that the wearer had just jumped one of the many small glacial crevasses we had been warned of. The lithium battery in my headlamp generated a bright light in the frigid night air, and I was glad I had made the investment to buy such a dependable battery. If you didn't have one of these batteries, you would definitely need a backup set—normal batteries went dead much sooner in the cold, and we had a solid five hours of night climbing before us. The mountain was no place to be without light. Being last, I was acutely aware of the darkness surrounding me, and had I not felt a tug on the rope from Mike, one of my scouts who was positioned immediately in front of me, I could have easily felt totally alone. With the tug, I stepped out onto the ice

We crossed the glacier and ensuing ridges in silence, except for the slight crunch of our crampons biting into the ice. After about three hours of steady climbing, we arrived at the base of Disappointment Cleaver, a large ridge of rock protruding through the ice and snow and running up the mountain's side for about a half a mile. Here we were to scramble up a broken rock wall to the spine of the ridge, which we would follow up to the next glacier. While waiting for our turn to mount the wall, I turned my light into the darkness at my right and let its beam search out a reflective surface. Nothing. The light evaporated into a black void. As far as I could tell, there was nothing but space to my right; the ridge was the lip of a precipice immense enough that I could not even see a glimmer of light reflecting off some valley floor below me. Twenty-feet ahead of me Mike was just starting to scramble up the broken rock wall when he vanished. A fraction of a second later I heard him call, "My light's gone out!" I located him with my light: he hadn't fallen.

"Get out your backup set," I called.

"I don't have any," he replied.

His response was quick and urgent. In an automatic response, I turned my head to look for someone close to Mike to help. Then I remembered that I was the last man of the last team and the only one who knew of Mike's predicament. I turned my light again upon Mike who was now trying to inch his way up the dark wall, trying to keep in step with the man who had just gone over the top of the wall and wasn't aware of what was going on behind him. I blurted an instantaneous decision, "Keep going. I'll use my light for both of us." And so while I jerked my headlamp beam up to Mike and back to the rock in front of me, we began to climb the rock wall.

With our senses intensely alert, we coordinated our movements until we were on top of the wall and near the spine of the cleaver. Here the various teams paused to rest and regroup. Fortunately, from this point on the going became somewhat easier since Mike could now slightly distinguish the path with the trail of headlamps stringing out in front of him. However, we still worked together since there were specific turns to negotiate and broken shale-like rock slides to avoid. Step by careful step, we treaded our way to the top of the cleaver, all the while concentrating on the trail that took us safely between the cliff on our right and the steep glacier to our left.

After about an hour, we saw the first hints of dawn appearing from our right. A short time later, Mike could see well enough on his own that he didn't need any more help from my light, and we both climbed more easily. We came to our resting spot, at the top of Disappointment Cleaver, and lay down exhausted but relieved, the sun's warmth and brightness now bathing us richly. We ate our small snack, savored a bit of rest, reflected briefly on our dark ordeal and then were up again and on our way.

Though intensely hard, the remainder of our climb passed without incident, and we summited. We joined with the rest of our group and exulted in our successful attempt. And from the view at the top, I could look down on Disappointment Cleaver and inwardly rejoice to know that a tragedy had been averted. But with a quiet jolt, I realized that a tragedy had been averted not only for Mike but for an entire team, for we had all been roped together—our every success or failure had been more connected than I had ever realized—my "brother's" welfare had been my very own.

2

The Discomfort Zone

Guideline: Activities that take us out of our comfort zone make
            us better students.
Insight: Adversity heightens our interest in learning from the
            Lord.

You Learn Best When It's Really, Really Cold

They wanted to live. I could see it in their eyes. However, most thought
they wouldn't make it through the night. The few that had any hope of
living were sure that they would come out of this with only limited use
of their extremities, if they had extremities at all after the amputations.
Through their unblinking, raptly focused eyes, I could see into their deep-
est thoughts: How did we come to this point? What mass lapse of sanity
fooled us into choosing to do this? We should have listened to our mothers.
But no. We're doomed. There is no way out. No escape. . . . And that is just
where I wanted them—just where I wanted my small group of twelve- and
thirteen-year-old scouts to be.

It was sheer luck that our campout in late February landed on the
coldest weekend of the year, of many years. Temperatures were forecast to
be less than ten degrees in the lowlands and, therefore, much colder in the
mountains. Perfect. But all were not as delighted as I was. Thursday night
my assistant scoutmaster called up.

"Mark, have you been listening to the weather report?"

"No," I replied.

"Well, the temperature is supposed to get down to only six or seven
degrees above zero," he said, emphasizing the word only.

"No kidding," I said. "Why, that's great. We'll probably qualify for at least a silver bead, maybe a gold."

Big pause.

"You're sick."

"No. I just lived most of my life near Canada."

"That just compounds your problem."

Realizing that trying to reason with a person who actually wanted to be thrown into the briar patch would be hopeless, my assistant scoutmaster decided to go on the campout, but maybe not so much to support the activity as to be there to help collect the bodies in the morning.

Friday afternoon arrived, and there was an amazing turnout: fifteen boys and five adults. They all met in my driveway. The boys looked like puffballs dressed in all the winter gear their families owned or could acquire from the local army surplus store. They all had their packs ready, straps tightened. No loose gear because on a hike loose gear means lost gear, and on a cold weather campout you don't want to be without anything. This was not a car campout. We were hiking in a little over a mile, so since all the gear had to be packed in with us we had pack inspection a couple of times. We loaded the gear in the trucks and vans, had our prayer, and headed up the canyon, a caravan into the white wilderness.

There was still a bit of daylight left when we reached the trailhead. We unloaded the vehicles, hoisted our gear, got everyone pointed in the right direction, positioned the leaders amongst the boys, and started up the trail to the campsite. We covered the distance in good time, and I noticed spirits were fairly high. Of course, that was due mainly to the fact that there was still some daylight. (On a cold weather campout light equals hope.)

The first order of business was to get the tents up. The various tent groups located their spots and started stomping the snow down to make nice level places on which to pitch their tents. Once that was done, the tents went up, the ground pads, sleeping bags, and gear were thrown inside, and the boys flocked to the campfire, crowding around and jockeying for prime space.

They were careful, though, not to get too close to the flames. The image of one of their friends who had accidentally shrink-wrapped himself in his nylon ski pants at an earlier campout was still fresh in their minds. They stood there cooking their hot dogs, gabbing and taunting each other—standard fare for twelve- and thirteen-year-olds around a campfire. In the light of that good-sized fire, they didn't notice the sun setting behind the mountains and the dark chill of a deep winter night surreptitiously creeping to within inches behind them. I believe they thought the fire would last forever. Wrong. As all fires do, it began to die down. They called for more wood, but no one wanted to leave the fire to get what little remained of the nighttime wood supply. The fire died down even more, and they began to feel the extreme cold at their backs. They huddled closer together.

I gathered the last few sticks from our nighttime fire supply and muscled my way up to the fire, placing them carefully on the diminishing flames. Then I announced that it was time for a short campfire program. We sang a couple of songs, yelled a couple of yells, told a couple of jokes, and then had the "scoutmaster's minute" (a time when I relate a brief story or share a few comments about a gospel principle). By the time the scoutmaster's minute was done, the fire was down to glowing embers and only a faint red glow reflected off the boys' faces as they crouched close to what scant heat struggled to leave the fire pit. The cold was now a dominating presence pressing firmly against all of us.

"Boys," I said. "Before we close, I want to review with you how to keep warm tonight." If there had been any rustling or chattering going on, it stopped then. Those usually frenetic grasshoppers sat as still as the frozen trees around them and riveted their attention upon me. It was then that I saw in their eyes that they wanted to live and were hoping I would tell them how. At this moment, they were oozing teachability. I owned their attention. Things that I had told them in the preceding weeks I was going to repeat to them now. But under the present circumstances, those recommendations would take on the status of almost divine revelation. I had them where I needed them.

As I reviewed the list of necessities and recommendations, I could almost see a mental chisel etching each item into their memories. Some even moved their lips, tacitly reciting each item: head up, feet down, loose dry socks, head cover, stay on your ground pad. When I finished reviewing the check list, they seemed almost disappointed—there needed to be more; there had to be more. They thought that maybe I had forgotten something critical to their survival. At that point they were so receptive that if I had told them that eating rotten worms would help them stay warm, they probably would have done so, and without a moment's hesitation. I thought, *So this is what it takes to finally and utterly grab our fickle human attention. Adversity sure makes us better students.* We closed with prayer and then dismissed. The scouts went directly to their tents and began preparing for bed in earnest.

I gave them about ten minutes, then began my rounds for a last check-in to make sure all were appropriately readied. To a person, every one had attended to every last detail. Secure with the knowledge that they were prepared, I went to my tent and prepared for the night.

In the morning, I arose to find one of the boys already up and trying to encourage the last night's darkened embers back into flame. I was impressed. I helped him get the fire going and then went around and checked all the tents. Most of the boys were in the process of awakening but didn't want to leave the warmth of their sleeping bags. Some boys, however, were still so deeply asleep, I actually had to perform a variety of professional wrestling techniques on their tents (with them still inside), and when that didn't work, I drew upon my bevy of animal stampede impersonations (an elephant stampede is the best) to get them going, so that breakfast and the day's events could get underway. These worked to some degree, but what worked best was an invitation to come and look at the reading on the digital thermometer we had brought with us.

Initially, it read minus three, but then while we watched, it dropped another degree to minus four. The boys and leaders alike cheered when they saw that. It was like we had just vanquished an ominous opponent.

After that, the day formally began with everyone once again gathering close about the fire, listening to basic instructions, and joining in morning prayer. As the boys headed off to get breakfast ready or to take care of general duties, the assistant scoutmaster came up to me and commented on making it through the night. He mentioned how amazingly attentive the boys had been at the campfire the previous night.

"Yeah," I said. "They thought they were all going to wake up dead."

"So did I," he said.

"You're kidding, even with that four-inch foam mattress and all the blankets and stuff?"

"I wanted to go out comfortably."

"Well, be that as it may, last night was kind of interesting. I think we just caught a firsthand glimpse of one of the Lord's most effective ways of catching our attention and making us listen to Him: imminent death, misery, or some other adversity. It makes us better students. Those boys were as focused as we'll ever see them."

My assistant scoutmaster paused and looked at me warily.

"If adversity makes us better students, then I assume we'll be going on a few more cold campouts."

"Most certainly, but not just cold campouts, really, really, really cold campouts."

"Really. I can hardly wait."

"I thought you'd like that. Oh, and by the way, did I mention I've lived most of my life near Canada?"

3

Wilderness Seclusion

Guideline: Use secluded wilderness environments to help foster unity and relationships.

Insight: The more we protect ourselves from worldly influences, the more heavenly our relationships will be.

A Tale of Two Parks
(or At Home in the Wilderness)

The young women of the ward wanted a super activity. They got one. With a motivated, dedicated Young Women's president encouraging them, the Beehive, Mia Maid, and Laurel leaders came up with an exciting activity—one that was a little bit city and a little bit country.

The first day was going to be spent at a local amusement park. It was no Disneyland, but it still offered a variety of fun rides and shows. The next day, it was up to the most scenic mountain lake in the area. But it wasn't the lake that was the destination, it was a little known natural water slide nearby. This slide was of seemingly mythical existence because you could only find out about it (and locate it) if you knew one of the locals. One of the girls knew a person who knew a person. To our amazement, despite being almost as difficult to obtain as a rainbow's pot of gold, she got the location and directions. The girl was so enthusiastic that she won over the imaginations of all the other girls—everyone wanted to go sliding down this wonder of the natural world. I was asked to go along as one of adult priesthood representatives.

The day the super activity started was beautiful. We left early and arrived at the amusement park just after it opened. Great start. We had maximized the time factor. We had hours and hours to enjoy the place. Standing in a group outside the ticket booths, we asked everyone if they would like to go around as a group.

"No. Let us go around on our own," the older girls insisted.

As if on cue, the rest of the group quickly sided with the older girls, and we had a cacophony of pleading and pouting. After quick deliberation, the leaders decided to let the group split up. The various leaders and moms would split up as well to go with the smaller groups. The girls banded together with their friends, forming large loosely knit cliques. We reminded everyone where to meet for lunch. As soon as the tickets were bought and hands were stamped, the girls sprinted away toward a variety of determined and undetermined destinations, moms and leaders chasing after to keep up.

At the first intersection with a signpost, however, previous parlays and promises about staying together went out the window as the groups began to disagree on the exact ride to go on first. Our main groups fractured into sub-group friendships that began heading off to whatever they wanted to do first. It appeared that keeping people even semi-together would be about as easy as herding grasshoppers with a bulldozer. We had about three hours till lunch, so hunger would reunite us. But that little window of opportunity was hardly a saving grace for any togetherness and relationship building. I was a bit dismayed that there would probably not be as much cross-group interaction, especially since some of the newer, younger girls were timid and less confident about expanding their social horizons.

The crowds built up fast and the lines began to get longer and longer. The rides were going non-stop. With the added surge in park patrons, the general din grew till the decibel level rivaled that of a fully packed and frenetic bowling alley. The roller coaster click-clacked and swooshed, the corkscrew rumbled, and the bumper cars crashed. On top of that was the ubiquitous screaming from frenzied thrill-riders. There was also the omni-present smell of hot dogs, popcorn, and cotton candy, not to mention general humanity. I'd been to the park a couple of times, so I chose the shows over the rides, but went out regularly to see if I could catch sight of any of the girls. For the next three hours, I rarely saw any.

Near lunchtime, some of the girls started showing up at our midday rendezvous point. They came in two here, three there, and occasionally one by one. They asked about lunch. I said, "Almost ready." A small group nearby had sat down and were mundanely chatting while pulling at the grass.

"So, how are the rides?" I said.

"Good," one offered.

Another said, "The corkscrew is the best. But I got dizzy, so I had to sit on the bench for a while. Emily almost threw up." Emily wasn't talking and didn't look up at the mention of her name.

More girls filtered in. Finally, most were there, so we passed out the lunches and drinks. During lunch we heard about escapades and thrills, "near-death" experiences, and crowds and lines. I noticed the girls had paired up in their usual groups. We had all gathered on a spot of grass a little apart from the pressing throng of the crowd. As they ate, I watched the Beehives talk and giggle, the Mia Maids talk and laugh while practicing their scoping-out-boys techniques, and the Laurels talk, critique the rides, and more boldly glance at the older teenage guys passing by, who might be eyeing them as well.

All of this was interesting to watch, but the intangible influence of the crowd was to my awareness causing a mood change: the girls were becoming less amiable than what I had seen earlier in the day when we were just preparing to enter the park. It probably had started earlier, but the effects were more obvious with everyone in one spot. The girls were behaving with more restraint and reservation. Previously animated conversations had become subdued, less spontaneous. One girl, who earlier in the day talked as much with her arms and hands as with her mouth, now confined herself to slight shrugs and discrete glances. Where there had been some intermixing between groups at the beginning, now there was less. The shyer girls had really faded. From the fringes, they just watched the more talkative girls.

As the girls finished lunch, they got into their respective alliances and began heading back out to the rides. There didn't seem to be much concern with meeting up with others along the way. They just wanted to go have fun with their exclusive groups. A few of the less socially adept left with what seemed to be a slight sense of resignation. As I watched these girls step into the crowd, there was a greater poignancy to their disappearing into the mass of people. They walked, as it were, condemned to be swept away without regard, disconnected from us and the rest of the group, by the passing rush of the crowd.

We had set a time in the later afternoon to regroup. I arrived at the spot about half an hour early and found some of the Beehives and Mia Maids already there.

"What are you guys doing here so early," I asked.

"We're tired. We're ready to go."

"Really, with all the rides and stuff?"

"Yeah, they're okay."

"Gee, I thought you'd be milking every last minute," I replied.

"No, we're done," a girl said rather listlessly.

"Well, okay," I offered. "You're sure you don't want to do a few more rides?"

"No, we're good."

Others began filtering in. Almost all returned early except for a few die-hard thrill seekers. There wasn't a lot of chatting. Maybe they were tired. Limited inquiries were made into how the day went unless it was for an immediate pal.

Some of the leaders did reconnaissance, and we rounded up everyone. It didn't take long to herd everyone to the cars; they went like horses to the barn at the end of a hard day. We headed home for dinner.

The next morning, we arose early since the drive to the natural water slide would take about two hours, especially since this was our first time. The drive through the forested hills and mountains was beautiful, but most of the girls didn't notice through their closed eyelids—late night.

As we turned off the paved road onto the dirt road that followed the creek back into the mountains, most everyone was jostled awake by the rough road.

"Where are we?" someone asked.

"I'm not sure, but I have an idea," I replied.

"Is this the right road?"

"Don't know for sure, but I think so." The girls and adults alike had their faces plastered against the windows looking up at the high mountain peaks and the blue sky above. The trees were so tall and dense that you had to wait for a clearing to get a good view. To our right side, a creek smashed and bashed its way down the ravine. The sun was up and glistening off the mist and wet rocks.

"How far do we go on this road," a girl in the back asked.

"Somewhere around five or six miles. Why? Do you get car sick?" I asked as I swerved to miss a pot hole.

"Maybe," she replied.

"Well, let me know way before you do," I said, emphasizing the word *way*.

"Is that the creek from the water slide?"

"Probably."

"It looks cold."

"Probably."

"Will we be able to find this place?"

"Probably."

The road began to steepen. It was dry and in most places wide enough for two cars, so we were able to negotiate it well and keep a reasonable speed of twenty miles per hour.

"Well, look at that. I think we're here," I said, squinting into the windshield.

"We're here?"

"Not the waterslide but the end of the road. We'll park, and from here on we hoof it."

"How far?"

"The person we talked to said about a mile from the end of the road."

There was only one other car at the trailhead.

Everyone was out of the cars putting on backpacks and at the same time craning their necks to look at the steep, forested slopes and massive granite outcroppings high above us.

"Which way?" asked one of the Young Women leaders.

"It looks like this old jeep road on the other side of the berm would be it," I replied while scoping out the trail from atop a boulder on top of the berm. I jumped down and said, "Let's go."

A couple of Young Women leaders came up front by me and the rest hung back behind the young women who were in a kind of loosely formed phalanx. For the first hundred yards or so, there wasn't too much talking because the girls were checking their surroundings as they passed through. With each step though, they became more acclimated.

I could tell most of the girls were unused to being far out into the woods. They commented on the beauty all around but didn't venture far from the group. The girls would form intermittent clusters around some of the adults to ask questions and then they would drift back into the phalanx. A few even came up front to visit with me to ask about the area and what I thought of the trail.

"Hey, Brother Harrison. Are there animals up here?"

"Tons, but you'll probably not see any because we're too big a group and we're making too much noise."

That answer gave some the green light to be more adventurous, and they began darting here and there to break off a branch or smell a flower. A few went over to the bank of the creek.

"Come over here," the girls at the bank yelled. "Look at the pools and waterfalls." We stopped hiking so we could all go see. We hopped down the bank to the granite creek bed that had been carved by glaciers thousands of years ago. The girls gazed into the crystal clear pools and watched the frothy splash coming and going from the pools. There were little skeeters darting about on the pool surface. One younger girl spotted some tiny fish.

"Hey, come look here," she cried.

Several girls, including even some of the older ones, joined her. Together, they all bent over trying to point out this fish and that.

"This is great, but let's keep going to the waterslides," I shouted, trying to be heard over the nearby cascades.

We herded and cajoled everyone back onto the trail. We hadn't walked far when we saw a man, a woman, and their two younger children coming toward us.

"Hello there. Is this the trail to the waterslides?" I asked

"Yeah, you're just about fifteen to twenty minutes away," the man replied.

"Is it easy to find?"

"You can't miss it. It's definitely worth the walk." He smiled and waved as he passed on by.

The girls, one after another, waved energetically, smiled, said hello and asked, "How much further?"—not because they were tired, but more out of friendly curiosity toward these newly discovered human creatures found in the wild. After amicable but repetitive grilling from the girls, the family finally escaped out the back end of our group.

We walked up the trail for another ten minutes. By now the girls were chattering, laughing, throwing clumps of weeds at each other, and doing some early pilfering of sack lunch items.

We came to a stream crossing, about twenty feet wide, slow moving and about a foot to a foot and a half deep. Since I anticipated getting my feet wet watersliding, I just stepped in to make the cross. I was stunned at how cold the water was.

"Ooo, that water's chilly," I exclaimed.

Then a little Beehive stepped in. She did one of those stop-action rigid poses—mouth and eyes wide open, no breathing. Then quick as a wink she sucked air, let out an off-the-chart high-pitched scream that mostly only dogs could hear, and promptly in double-time pranced on top of the water to the other side. Seeing that, the other girls decided to try to cross by stepping on rocks. That didn't work so well because it became a game with some of the girls to see if they could distract the crosser into miss-stepping and ending up in the water. It worked several times. A few crashed and splashed and the spectators hooted and laughed.

After watching this for a while, I went up the trail another hundred yards where the trees to my left ended. Beyond this, there was a large open slope. When I got to the edge of the trees where the trail disappeared, I went slack-jawed. There before me was a gently rolling granite slope about two hundred feet long and fifty feet wide and covered in an almost uniform half inch of water that spread over it, beginning at the top where the creek we had been following spilled out from a pool and over the slope. Nothing I had ever seen, man-made or nature-made, rivaled this. Near the bottom there was even a three foot wide by one foot deep water-filled depression that ran from side to side to serve as a natural stopping point. A few of the girls caught up to me, took a look, and started yelling and waving to the others below that we had found it and to hurry up.

We stepped onto the surface letting the water envelope our feet, and cautiously, so as not to slip, crossed to the other side where there were some big dry spots where we could lay out our towels and drop our gear. More arrived at the slide, and we heard the hurrahs as they saw the slide.

A couple of the Mia Maids and a Beehive were ready in a flash, and we ran up the dry section to the top of the slide. We looked down the slope and hollered to the others to take a look at us, the first ones to go down. Even in our adrenalized excitement one thing caught our attention—the water, the c-o-o-l-d water. Even though the sun was shinning and the temperature was probably in the upper 70s, the water felt like ice. Well, it probably was just a couple of degrees above ice. The girls who were gathered at the top all looked at me.

I looked back at them and said, "Man, this is cold."

They all nodded with big smiles and replied, "Yeah, you go first."

We had come this far, so I gingerly sat down, letting the water first touch my feet, then my calves, then my upper legs, and then my bottom.

"Whoa," I cried. Then with a rebel yell, I shoved off and went sliding down.

Within a second, I forgot the cold and just enjoyed sliding and picking my path. I hit the water-filled natural depression and let out a war cry when that cold water sprayed all over me. I stood up quickly and yelled, "That was great. I'm goin' again."

By now, quite a group of the girls were at the top huddled together, waiting for the next brave soul. At this point, age had no bearing. It was all just guts.

One of the Mia Maids moved to the center of the slide and pronounced, "Okay, I'm going." She sat down, did a quick shiver, shoved off with a scream, and headed down. The girls at the top cheered. As soon as the Mia Maid splashed into the water-filled depression, she shot to her feet at the speed of light, turned and with a big, bug-eyed look of cold-induced horror screamed at the top of her lungs. The girls all laughed. She laughed back at them and then started running to the top to go down again. That broke the ice (so to speak) and the urging and coaxing at the top became more animated. Deals were struck right and left:

"Okay, I'll go if you go."

"I'll go after you go."

"Let's go together, but you go first."

They started sliding down. Each one got cheered by the rest. When anyone splashed into the depression, all cheered. As each slider jumped up, no matter who, she would look at the group with a shocked expression, laugh and be joined by all the others laughing too. Soon groups started going down together. It didn't matter who knew whom. It was just who would go. There was a group of Laurels with a small shivering Beehive. There were groups of Mia Maids, Beehives, and Laurels, and there were groups of girls and leaders. They laughed, screamed, and splashed together.

This continued for almost two hours. Exertion and the cold water finally persuaded most to sit on their towels out in the sun to warm up. Some had to stop because they had worn thin the hind end of their bathing suits from sliding down the granite—an unforeseen side effect from sliding down rock, albeit smooth rock. The girls talked and teased each other about stunts, funny grimaces, blue lips, and chattering teeth.

All by themselves in this beautiful primeval place, sheltered by the trees, the cascading creek, and the mountains around, it was good to see them enjoying each other, liking each other. Only those who were present could share in these conversations and enjoy future references to this idyllic scene and enjoyable time. By the smiles on their faces and the comfortable conversations amongst any and all, this group had relaxed, had become content with itself. I smiled as I noticed the harmony and comfort felt by all: the timid, gregarious, and peculiar alike.

When the sun started to set, the leaders said it was time to head back to the cars. Many girls slowly gathered their belongings, reluctant to leave. But we were getting a little hungry. The sun was not too far from going down, and there were no facilities—a big factor convincing lingerers to leave. So, people laced on shoes, packed up, and started heading back down the trail. There was a casual ease to everyone's pace. People were tired but smiling. Conversation was subdued and pleasant. The aroma from the trees and plants still infused our senses. By the time we arrived at the cars, the coolness of the evening had begun to settle in the shadows.

As we got into the cars, I took a last look around at the dark green, forested mountainsides and the treetops up the narrow valley where we had just spent the afternoon. I felt like waving a fond good-bye to this place that had taken us in and provided us an atmosphere in which our group could be comfortable enough to grow together. As I reflected on the experience of the day prior, I thought it had almost been a waste compared to this. And based on that, I thought (like the poet Wordsworth) that maybe the world is sometimes too much with us and that we need to distance ourselves from it occasionally so that we can blossom, like our Young Women group did, in the seclusion of that wilderness wonderland park—a place where our group, sheltered as it was from worldly observation and distraction, found a piece of heaven on earth that in turn allowed all to be, especially in a heavenly sense, more at home.

4

Ups and Downs

Guideline: Hiking can teach how to distinguish between good and
bad pathways.
Insight: Going up is hard for us, but going down is hard on us.

Downhill, the Great Deceit

I was coming down the mountain along with the rest of our youth group from a high mountain lake, Lake Hardy. It had been a long steep hike up, and it was a long steep hike down. I had done just fine until about halfway down when my right knee started to stiffen from all the pounding and jolting, causing me steady discomfort mixed with occasional sharp, debilitating pain. I thought to myself, *Not again*. I hate going downhill. My body always gets beaten up going downhill. *I'd rather go uphill all day long. It's hard, but at least I don't get hammered.*

When, at last, we got to a more level section where my knee was not being so punished, I thought back on my painful descent and the mental comment I had made about going downhill. As my mind wandered, I reviewed the hikes I'd been on over the last fifteen years or so and realized that I had rarely ever been hurt going up, but that I could remember a variety of times where I or one of the youth had been hurt or beaten up coming down. I thought, *How interesting that on almost any given hike, we always long for the downhill part, but it's usually the downhill part where we suffer injury or pain the most.* The more I thought about it, the more I realized that I had seen this pattern for a long time but had not given it a second thought.

I recalled an incident from years earlier at Harrison Lake, a lake high in the Idaho Selkirks, in which a young man heading down the trail from the lake had met with a small disaster as we were returning to the cars at the trailhead. It had been a backpacking hike, about three miles one way, involving a significant elevation gain in a short distance.

As we descended, some of the older boys began running down the trail, despite their heavy and hastily secured pack loads. This young man decided to do the same. Before he had gone too far, I yelled for him to stop and reminded him that running down the trail was not a good idea—he might fall and hurt himself. Half listening, he nodded and then began walking and then walking faster and faster down the trail until he was out of sight around the next bend. It wasn't but a few minutes before I found him lying to the side of the trail, scuffed up and bruised. His face was covered with embedded dirt and pine needles. He was sniffling and crying slightly, and he welcomed my rescue. I didn't need to ask what had happened. It was obvious. He had started running down the trail again, had tripped on a root or rock, and had plunged face first into the trail with his heavy pack on top of him. I dusted him off, cleaned and treated his face, and sent him off again down the trail. This time, however, my repeated cautions were more humbly heeded, and he kept to a moderate and controlled amble for the rest of the way back.

Time passed, and many hikes and backpacking trips came and went, including my Lake Hardy experience, before I found myself readying some youth for a training hike for an upcoming fifty-miler. I had planned a five mile hike, one way, to a high mountain lake in the Wasatch Mountains. The first three and a half miles were level with a good wide trail. However, the next mile was steep, rutted, strewn with bowling-ball-sized rocks, and gained about 1200 feet in vertical elevation in that distance. Then the trail leveled out and finished in beautiful aspens, pines, and grassy meadows.

The group covered the first part of the hike with no problem. But as we began going up, it wasn't five minutes before I heard the first murmurings: "When are we going to get there? I need to rest again. How much farther?" I listened, smiled, and told them, "Just around the bend." Actually, after about twenty minutes, I didn't hear any comments, probably because speaking took too much energy, and it's pretty hard to talk when you're inhaling every air molecule in a ten-foot radius as fast as you can. About halfway up, we stopped for a long rest. Some of the group began to talk about the next day's return trip and how good it would be to be going down this trail. I listened to their comments for a couple of minutes, then mentioned something that just spontaneously fell out of my mouth and that has since become kind of a mantra of mine. I said, "Gang, let me just say that going up may be hard for you, but going down is hard on you." They looked at me with that "what planet are you from?" look. Well, after a few more minutes we hoisted our packs and started back up the mountain to the lake. We arrived at the lake at dusk, just as a storm was starting to rage around us. Interestingly, despite how tired they were, every youth was able to muster the energy to hustle and get his tent up quickly before too much rain had hit us. We waited out the storm in our tents. It wasn't too long before the storm passed, as is usual with weather patterns in the high mountains. We had dinner, a little campfire time, enjoyed stargazing, and then hit the sack.

When morning came, we awoke to a crisp, beautiful day. We enjoyed a quick breakfast, explored the small lake, waded and swam briefly (very briefly, the water was still pretty cold), and then packed up about lunch-time and started back down the trail. Spirits were pretty high; this was going to be the easy part—the downhill part. For the first quarter of a mile or so, the trail was broad and gently sloped, surrounded by grasses, flowers, and alpine trees. Everyone was talking, teasing, laughing, and stepping along briskly. This was paradise: no burning, over-taxed muscles; no rapid gasping for air; no salty sweat running down our faces and stinging our eyes. We could enjoy the vistas easily and without distraction . Gravity had changed allegiances—yesterday's foe had become today's friend. Even our packs were hardly noticeable. Thus we continued down. We hardly noticed the steepening pitch except that we had to be a little more aware of our footing, but not enough so as to mar our delight in going down.

Then the trail steepened sharply. It wasn't too much of a problem at first; we just had to keep the brakes on. Soon, however, the trail became rutted and rocky, besides being steep. After not more than a few hundred feet of trying to keep our footing and our balance, our leg muscles began to burn, but that was okay, still no labored lungs. A little farther down, the constant strain on the ligaments, tendons, and joints began to take its toll. Some began to slip; a few fell. Toes jammed hard into the front of boots. Skin rubbed hard against skin, became raw, and turned into blisters. Saintly gravity changed to a merciless demon as joints were pounded and tired muscles jarred, increasing the threat of more serious injuries like sprained ankles or twisted knees.

By the time we reached the bottom of the steep section, the group wasn't out of breath, but they were beaten up. Joints and muscles had been strained beyond being sore. Everyone walked, or rather shuffled. On the last part of the way back—the level, easy part—even the hardiest of the group plodded heavily along. In fact, one boy was so worn out that when he got to within fifty feet of the cars, he tripped on a pebble no bigger than the size of a marble and fell face first in the dirt, hardly able to rise. Another youth with whom I was walking was so battered by the hike down that when we got to an almost imperceptively small rise in the trail just two hundred feet from the cars, he turned to me and very desperately cried, "You didn't say there was still uphill."

When everyone got back to the cars and unloaded their packs, we just sank down onto the dirt or collapsed against a car fender. If a storm had hit us then, like what had happened to us when we had arrived at the lake, there would have been no way, in our present condition, that we could have set up our tents. We would have just sat in the rain, letting it drench us at will. At this point, through my fatigue, I saw something of a teaching moment, so I said, "Well, maybe you understand what I said before that going up is hard for us, but that going down is hard on us." There were just a few mumbled grunts, a few head nods, but no disagreements, and I think at that time all were beginning to see that going downhill could have a dark side.

Since then, the "hard for us, hard on us" couplet has been a catalyst for lessons and casual chats with leaders and youth. From such reflective discussions, certain scriptures have come to life for me, in particular 2 Nephi 28:21: "And others will he pacify, and lull them away into carnal security, that they will say: All is well in Zion; yea, Zion prospereth, all is well—and thus the devil cheateth their souls, and leadeth them away carefully down to hell."

The phrase "all is well—and thus the devil cheateth their souls, and leadeth them away carefully down to hell" especially hit home. Our experience going down from that high, Wasatch Mountain lake from its blissful beginning to its hurt and damaged end was that phrase's mirror image. Through that experience, I saw how carefully and deceitfully clever Satan will be in leading us to the point of significant spiritual damage. He will blind us to his designed destination with initial goodness and ease, worsening the circumstances ever so slightly, until we are at the point where we can hardly continue, or even worse, to a point where we feel unable to continue. It also reawakened me to the concept that heaven is up and hell is down. As long as we are going up, we are in the process of strengthening muscles and stamina, in spiritual terms, becoming more capable sons and daughters of God. While going down, we are in the process of hurting or even destroying ourselves, just what the devil would love—more beings in the same condition he is in.

So now, as I plod on through life toward that spiritual mountain lake or peak, I try to keep myself more aware and more wary of those deceitful downhills that distract me from the upward course. And in my plodding process I find the little couplet regularly comes in handy, helping me to stay focused on the proper path and to keep the right perspective. Therefore, if you happen to be standing quite near during a particularly stiff uphill type of day and hear me mutter something under my breath repeatedly and rapidly, don't cover your ears, it's probably just:

"Going up is hard for me; going down is hard on me.

"Going up is hard for me; going down . . . is hard on me."

5

Mountain Top Perspective

Guideline: Climbing to mountain tops can teach about the temple.

Insight: To be taught from on high is to be given greater perspective.

High on a Mountain Top

Some years back, I was told by my seventeen-year-old son that he and some of his friends had been talking about their favorite camping trips. One of the boys volunteered that when he was younger, he just wanted to go on the easy hikes and didn't like having to head up the mountain to visit the distant peaks and lakes, but that now as he thought about it, it was the hikes up to the high lakes and peaks that were the best ones. I smiled to hear the comment, especially as I found out who had said it. I noted that he had specifically referred to peaks and high lakes. And I wondered what it was that made this young man do so. I had always liked going up higher and farther but had never really identified why. I believed that to some degree it was more of an adventure to go where few others had been, to see what few others had seen. But as I pondered it further, I wondered if there was something more transcendent to my son's and my scout's sentiments.

Time went on, and the troop and I continued to hike high and far, but then we did one hike which unlocked, for me, some of the more subtle reasons why I am drawn to higher places.

We had climbed near to the top of an unnamed peak in northern Idaho. It was July, and we were hot and thirsty. I spied a small snow patch on top of a car-sized boulder near the top. The sun was shining brightly and the snow was melting fast. I studied the boulder, the snow, the slant and rapidity of the runoff and decided that the chance for impurities was negligible, so I leaned down and placed my sun-baked lips into the water coming down the granite surface and swallowed, swallowed again, and then kept swallowing. I can't remember tasting water so crisp, clear, and clean. My lips were almost numb because I was drinking out of the runoff only six or seven inches away from the snow, but the water was so sweet, I drank on. Then each of the scouts took a drink, and we filled our canteens there.

Refreshed, we climbed to the top of the peak to stare almost slack-jawed at what lay before us. We could see mountains and valleys extending into Canada, Montana, Idaho, and Washington. The valley air below had been a bit hazy, but from where we stood we looked through untainted air to behold, with almost perfect clarity, the panorama surrounding us. The view was unblemished. Clear air and elevation provided an exquisite perspective for a complete 360 degrees. Everything was more visible, more distinguishable: granite peaks, small glaciers, talus falls, deep green forests on mountain slopes, cascading streams, thin waterfalls, deep gorges, distant lakes. It had a marked effect on all of us, and after everyone's spontaneous gasps, even the noisiest of the young boys looked about in quiet awe. There have been times when the beauty has been so inspiring and the feeling so serene that I have spoken in only a whisper, so as not to desecrate the almost holy feeling of the wilderness about me. This was one of those moments. The quiet awe lasted for a while, and then I heard, "This is awesome," or "cool," or simply ". . . dude." I especially liked "dude." It ranked as one of the highest compliments in my scouts' vocabulary. We stayed up there soaking up the vista, satiating our senses until it was time to return to camp.

On the way back down, we stopped by the snow patch, drank, and refilled our canteens. That water was so good that even as we got back to camp most of the boys treasured it more than their soda pop. I, too, guarded mine trying to make it last as long as possible. Situated comfortably back at camp, we then had time to explore around the lake, fish, or just sit and enjoy a balmy evening. Once the boys were all engaged in one activity or another, I had a bit of time, so I chose to just sit. While quietly enjoying my surroundings, I was treated to an occasional swirl of breeze, untainted by anything man-made, that would bring a puff of pungent pine aroma past me so thick and delicious that I almost reeled in delirium. I also noticed that in that rarefied air I could hear more keenly: I could tune into the boys' conversations from clear across the lake, understanding their every word and sentence, whispered or otherwise. Some of the boys chose to swim in the chill lake water because it was so unusual to swim in water so clear and fresh. It was easy to see the bottom of the lake even in the very deep parts. As night came on, we gathered around the fire for dinner. Being so far removed from any commonplace dining situation, in our high mountain wooded grove, we ate the items we'd brought from home and savored them with heightened satisfaction and appreciation. Though no trained chef had prepared our fare, we all leaned back, rubbed our tummies, and wished for more. Finally, night was upon us, and we prepared to bed down. As we crawled into our sleeping bags, we closed our eyes upon a clear midnight sky strewn with a myriad of sparkling stars.

The next morning, we arose to the sun rising on the eastern horizon, shining brightly and coaxing the chill from the morning. Our schedule did not allow us to tarry about, so we packed up shortly after breakfast and prepared to head back. When we left, we left smiling, both on the outside and on the inside. This had been a quintessential experience—being there in that setting, we had been happy, even edified.

As time passed, I was released as scoutmaster and called to serve on the high council. During one of my first high council meetings, the stake president was leading a discussion on temple attendance. He emphasized that the members needed to have a "mountain top" experience. In the course of the discussion, he asked why temples are compared to mountains. A reflective pause followed the question while all contemplated an answer. The picture of that mountain in northern Idaho came to mind with me below it, looking up at it, and then me on top of the mountain, looking out from it. I suddenly saw a correlation. I raised my hand and said, "President, from the base of a mountain you are awed by its grandeur and majesty. With the effort it takes to get to the top, once there, you enjoy a greater perspective. To me, a temple experience is much the same. From the outside it is inspiring and majestic. After being in the temple and exerting the effort to learn there, you gain spiritual perspective." That was the first I had seriously thought of any similarities between temples and mountains, and it prompted an interest in seeking an awareness of others. And so, for the next while, I strove to understand other parallels between temples and mountains with the experience on that northern Idaho peak being the template for the comparison.

Some parallels came quickly. Others took more time, but first on my list was that mountains, especially mountain peaks, convey the idea of being closer to God, reminiscent of the closer-to-God feeling we have when in the temple. Being on a mountain positions us far from the common, lived-on surface of earth to a point reaching high into the sky. We feel farther from this telestial sphere and closer to the celestial bodies above, closer to the God in heaven, just as we are so positioned in the temple, the Lord's House on earth, a specific dwelling place for the Lord, which indeed places us close to Him.

Next, when in the mountains, being literally far from the hectic aspects of this earth life, we feel a greater peace and serenity, a parallel to the feeling we have when we step through the doors of the temple and shut out the world behind. Getting to the mountains typically removes us far from the helter-skelter stresses of daily life. Without those influences, our mental and emotional states can relax and a sense of peace can pervade. I once saw a billboard outside of Banff in the Canadian Rockies that stated, ". . . And the mountains shall bring peace unto the people." I wondered if the unknown author were LDS and if he were referring to just earthly mountains.

Further, mountain heights are generally places where the elements are cleaner and purer, an aspect that parallels the idea of the holiness found in the temple. We found pure water to drink, clear lakes to swim in, and clean air to breath on that north Idaho peak. In this I was reminded of temples where are found clean environs, a greater purity in the lives of those serving, and clearer perspective to aid in understanding eternal truths.

And finally, as can be so common after being in the temple, I frequently come away from a mountain peak edified for having been there.

Maybe it is because of these shared characteristics between temples and mountains that the Lord uses mountains frequently as places where He would instruct His prophets when there was no temple available. Prophets like Moses, Enoch, and Nephi all had mountain top learning experiences. By speaking to His prophets from the mountain tops, the Lord was emphasizing that they were being taught from "on high." I note with interest that the Savior taught his greatest sermon, the Sermon on the Mount, on a mount, again implying symbolically to His audience that they were being taught by a higher authority, indeed by the Most High.

There are, assuredly, other parallels, but the ones I have mentioned are the most significant for me. Nonetheless, I remain fascinated as each new discovery reveals what kindred spirits temples and mountains are.

Therefore, I continue to visit both as often as I can. And when I happen to head into the mountains with those who have not yet been to the temple, I take them hoping that they might enjoy not only the outdoor mountain experience but that they might also glimpse what their future temple experience will resemble: like being high on a mountain top.

6

Wilderness Rx

Guideline: Being in the wilderness can strengthen against spiritual apathy.

Insight: When the world is too much with us, we forget to seek the beauty of the Light that is so available to us.

Smog Dwellers

The weatherman called it haze, but really it was just dirty air. Then the fog set in. The result was smog—smog that lasted for weeks. I hate smog. I feel that every breath hastens death.

One thing I like to do is to explore the locally accessible areas for new hikes and camping spots. I do so for two reasons. First, it's just fun to get away and go exploring. Second, it gives me a heads-up on a location's possibilities and how they can help a campout be more successful. One day I had a little extra time in the morning, so I got up early, put my snowshoes in the car, and prepared my daypack.

I started driving toward the mouth of the canyon. Visibility was a hundred yards or so. It was cold enough that the fog had frozen to the bushes and trees like a silvery frosting. But despite the fairyland effect, the grayish brown air still cast a somber pall over everything. I drove slowly up the canyon, exercising extra caution in the winter conditions. The smog didn't seem to be thinning. *Oh well*, I thought, *at least I'll enjoy the exercise and the exploring.*

I kept driving up the two-lane road next to a rollicking mid-sized creek. I came through an archway of low-hanging tree branches and suddenly the smog became bright and somewhat translucent, like effervescent, glowing chiffon. I had to squint. I wondered how long I would have to deal with this blinding condition when all of a sudden I burst out from the smog to see a clear baby blue sky, sharply defined mountain ridges, darkly forested mountain slopes, and abundant sunshine everywhere. I leaned forward with my face almost over the steering wheel. "Wo-a-a-h." My smile just about split my head in half. I had been cooped up in that smog for so long, never really seeing the sun, just seeing shades of brownish gray, that I had never expected to see something like this. I hurried up the road to the parking area, jumped out of the car, threw on my snowshoes, and headed out across the snowfields at a happy gallop.

I covered a lot of ground fast. It was so good to be free of the smog and to be able to breathe clear, clean, beautiful air. Visually, I gulped down the glistening white snow and forest green scenery all around me. I explored for as long as I possibly could, squeezing in every last foray till it was past time to leave.

Returning to the car, I stowed my gear and just sat for a minute. I wanted to linger a moment longer in the joy of the environment and the experience. The moment came and went all too quickly, especially with the needs of the day pressing hard about me, so resignedly, I started the engine, turned the car about, and headed back down the canyon.

Traveling down the canyon, I could occasionally catch glimpses of the massive smog cloud smothering the valley beneath. I came to the border of the cloud, which on the way up had looked like luminescent chiffon, but which from this direction was a fairly defined wall of grayness. I took a deep breath, like I was jumping into the water, and then drove the car into the smog cloud.

Within a few hundred feet, a bright day turned nearly to night. I had to turn on the lights to see and to be seen. I continued deeper into the smog till I reached the valley floor and my home.

For the rest of the day I kept mentally replaying the pleasure of leaving the smog and breaking into the light. I felt like I had found a paradise, my own Shangri-La, a kind of secret treasure, and I could hardly wait to get back.

The next morning, I was up early so I could ready my gear and head back up the canyon.

I drove through the smog till I burst through the luminescent curtain and once again into paradise. Again, I stayed there searching out good camping spots as long as I could. All too soon, the time to leave came, and I had to return to the car and head back down the canyon.

Heading down the canyon road, I once again saw the massive smog cloud. I winced at the thought of having to go back into it. However, this time as I contemplated going back into the ominous gray-brown mass, I not only winced for myself, but also for all the thousands of other people who had to live in it too. They were working, walking, playing, existing in that rank mist, and most had no idea of how near the sunshine, blue sky, and clean air were to them. I decided that I needed to get the good word out. People needed to know that they didn't just have to go on living in the smog until it moved on or finally blew away (which didn't look like it was going to happen any time soon). Getting the news out might mean a lot more traffic on the canyon roads, but all of the happy faces would make it worthwhile. Knowing the truth could make them free from their smoggy-brown world, if only for just an occasional respite.

"Guess what?" I said as I burst into the kitchen from the garage. My wife turned from doing the breakfast dishes.

"So, did you have a good time checking out camping spots?" she asked.

"Yes," and without taking a breath I said, "we can't be the only ones who know that clean air, sunshine, and paradise are so near."

"Yes. What are you proposing?"

"Well, everyone knows that this air is heavily polluted: health alerts, respiratory problems, pollution by the mouthful, so I'm going on a campaign to get the word out that relief is just a short distance away. I think once people know that they aren't definitely trapped, they'll shout for joy, jump in their cars, and flock in droves to get out of this stuff."

As soon as I got to work, I let the girl at the front desk know about my discovery. She gave her head a thoughtful nod and was about to say something when a call came in—the momentum of the conversation died. I visited with a few of my coworkers on the way to my desk. The responses were mixed—everything from, "Amazing, I'd like to see that" to a simple "Hmm." Throughout the day, everyone I had any contact with heard about the world beyond the smog. I energetically beckoned and persuaded, pushing the cause. By the time Saturday rolled around, I had alerted a lot of people to the wonderful world beyond the smog, but as Saturday closed, only my wife, two friends, and a coworker had ventured up the canyons. So far, the truth had been declared, but not many had freed themselves of the smog.

Ultimately, a few others began heading up out of the smog to the bright, clean, clear, rejuvenating world beyond. There were more cars on the road and at the trailhead parking lot. Occasionally, I'd see a few cross-country skiing or snowshoeing. I'd wave and say, "Nice day, isn't it?" They'd wave back and say, "Beautiful. It doesn't get any better." But the vast majority of people in the valley seemed content to live their lives in the smog. They knew the smog was harmful, but most had become indifferent to it because life remained reasonably livable.

It seems that dwelling in the dark smog too long makes it hard to remember the benefits of the light. In fact, living in the dark too long seems to damage one's sense of wonder for the light. It made me feel kind of sad for all who never left the smog, all those who had become impassive before the light.

By the time of the next campout, I had spent lots of time up in the mountains and had found a great spot. The weather up high was beautiful. The boys had a great time in the sunshine, clean air, and beautiful white snow. We reveled in the experience of being in this white, light-filled paradise. I watched and smiled to see them laughing and playing, competing in the various events we had planned. It was good to be camping in the light. Maybe it was my imagination, but the boys seemed more alive than I had seen them in a while. I think that subconsciously, even spiritually, they were reacting to being out of the darkness in the valley. And though they might not have been as articulately appreciative of the difference between the smog world and this paradise, from their smiles I believed that this experience was being absorbed as a sort of inoculation against a time when they might be tempted, literally or spiritually, to stay in the smog—tempted not to seek even for a quick visit, the bright, clean, wonderful world—tempted to be impassive before the light.

7

Testimony Fire

Guideline: Use wilderness fire building to teach the importance of having a testimony.

Insight: We can best be a "light unto the world" by providing our own fire.

Campfire Therapy:
Light and Warmth

"Brother Harrison? Do you think you can get a fire going?" asked a scout next to me who was holding a small box of matches in his hand. His inquiry was very earnest.

It was November, the troop's first truly winterlike campout, and we had just hiked up a canyon for a mile and a half in pretty deep snow. The snow at our campsite, which was amongst some big pine and spruce trees, was about three feet deep. In the open areas, it was deeper. The temperature was a few degrees below freezing.

"Oh, I think so," I replied.

"I hope so," the young scout countered. "I'm starting to get a little cold and hungry."

"Me too," I said. "Say, hand me another match. The first one didn't take hold."

The scout fingered out a few matches from the box, dropped a couple in the snow and handed me a couple more. Other scouts who had finished setting up their tent sites and stowing their gear began to gather around. For most of them, this was their first snow campout not right by a car and not part of a massive Klondike Derby. As long as they had stayed busy, they had stayed warm. But now most of the work was done, so they began wandering over. As their exertions stopped, so did their heat output, and they started to feel the chill.

The second match got a little more fire from the try, but still didn't get things going. I rearranged the kindling and added some more tinder. The scouts began to gather around, guardedly hopeful, but skeptical that a real fire could actually be made in such deep snow, at night, and in the night-time cold, which as everyone knows is colder than daytime cold. I looked up at them and saw in their faces that they were putting all their trust and hope in my ability to make a fire. Usually, if someone doesn't succeed on the first couple of tries to get a fire going, there are two or three others at his elbow eagerly vying for the chance to prove they can. In this case, however, there was no jostling for a chance to be the "pyro-hero." All just looked coldly, stoically on. At this point, the capacity for generating light and warmth did not seem to be in them. They looked to me with what faith they could muster that fire could be started in these conditions. Knowing what a fire meant to the comfort and well-being of everyone, I felt a certain stress to get this fire going. A doubtful thought as to my ability momentarily crossed my mind, causing me a quick bit of slight panic. I dismissed the thought. Fire building was a strength of mine. I refocused and finished my preparations.

I struck another match, positioned it in the tinder, and saw a flame take to the tinder. Soon more tinder began to ignite. Then the kindling began to catch and finally the larger pieces. As the flames grew and began dispelling darkness, the boys' countenances changed. It was like watching in slow motion the facial actions to the words of the primary song: "No one likes a frowny face . . . " The corners of their mouths turned up, their cheeks raised, and then their eyes widened and gleamed. It was the clearest physical manifestation of hope acquisition that I had ever seen. I added more wood, and then others did so too.

Soon the boys were positioning themselves comfortably around the fire, even taking off their heavier outer coats. They leaned forward, placing their hands near the fire. Some positioned their feet near the fire although this usually isn't a good idea because one doesn't feel his feet warming till after the shoe has began to melt. I passed out some cookies and crackers and hot water for hot chocolate.

After they downed a few handfuls, one of the older boys said, "Brother Harrison, this is turning out a lot better than I thought it would."

I smiled and said, "Good. I'm glad you think so. I'm liking it too. Nice to have a fire, isn't it?"

He grinned with a cookie half stuffed in his mouth and nodded.

I looked at the fire and thought how much we owed to the light and warmth of that fire. I reflected for a moment on how grateful I was that I had the skill and experience to make that fire. I was glad that I could bring light and warmth when others felt unable to do so for themselves. They leaned on me for the present, and I was good with that.

Later, while in my tent nestled comfortably in my sleeping bag, I thought back on the fire building episode of that night. It reminded me of when I had been in my scouts' shoes many years earlier on rainy, cold campouts in the Cascade mountains, relying on someone else's knowledge and skill to build a fire for me and provide the light and warmth I yearned for. I remembered when I had finally acquired the ability to make fire in most any condition, with or without matches, and how that knowledge changed me, how much more secure and confident I felt knowing that I could provide light and warmth for myself and others, if need be, even in dire circumstances. Once that capacity resided in me, I didn't have to lean on anyone else for basic light and warmth. Even more important, however, I could provide for others, and eventually help them acquire that same knowledge and confidence for themselves.

I've heard that we cannot stand on borrowed light. How true that is, especially if knowing how to make fire for light and warmth is akin to having a testimony. Providing one's testimony for others to lean on is certainly important at one point, but how much more important to help develop that knowledge in others that they might benefit for much longer than a momentary encounter with light and warmth.

My young scouts that night had enjoyed borrowed light and warmth. Eventually, they learned and acquired the capacity to enjoy light and warmth that they themselves could provide, and not only in a physical sense by being able to build a real fire, but spiritually, through testimonies they developed that provided light and warmth for themselves and others, especially in the mission field.

I'm sure there will come a time in their lives, as it has in mine and in most everyone's life, when life's cold and snowy nights will threaten. Those scouts may not only have to sustain themselves through such ordeals, but others as well. But I think they'll do all right because they're prepared, just like the scout motto says to be. And whether they need to apply their preparedness to make a fire in a physical sense or a spiritual one, they'll provide a pretty nice campfire, and around it there will be a lot of happy, grateful campers, not to mention themselves, enjoying some light and warmth—some campfire therapy.

8

Fifty-Milers

Guideline: Fifty-mile hikes prepare youth for missions.
Insight: Youth can grow emotionally and mentally, develop self-reliance, find power in prayer, and gain confidence to endure to the end.

The Fifty-Miler

The fifty-mile hike is an adventure. It takes youth and their leaders deep into the wilderness to areas seldom seen and even less seldom experienced. There are sights and wonders of creation that awe and inspire. It gives one the opportunity to feel close to nature and its maker. The air is cleaner, the water purer, and the smells from trees and flowers more noticeable. More important, however, a fifty-miler can tremendously benefit, spiritually and otherwise, our youth who complete one. From the seven fifty-milers that I have done, I have come to see this extended hike as an amazingly effective and unique tool available to our youth programs.

First, those who embark upon and complete a fifty-miler gain ground on the pathway to maturity. They spend a lot of time mingling and interacting. And they learn to respond to the close proximity of friends, acquaintances, leaders, and possibly fathers. On such a hike, it is a lot of fun being together, but inevitably there will be instances where the youth will have to learn respect, tolerance, patience, sacrifice, or thoughtfulness.

On my first fifty-miler, I saw a relationship grow between three deacon-aged friends who tented together. From there, their relationship evolved into one of the strongest bonds that I've seen among quorum members. Such a strong friendship developed that they became known as "the three musketeers," and truly adhered to the motto: All for one, and one for all. They supported each other, encouraged each other, and followed each other in good habits and actions. All three became Eagle Scouts, served honorable missions, and married in the temple. On that hike, however, they had to learn to tolerate one another's opinions, or philosophies as they called them; they had to practice patience waiting for a friend to catch up or do his part of the tent chores; and they had to practice sacrifice and patience when it came to sharing or trading food items, which is one of the hardest things to do out on the trail when food is precious and metabolic rates are rampant. Certainly, these virtues weren't perfected on the hike, but these young men set a precedent there. From such brotherhood, or "quorumhood," one can begin to understand how the quorum relationship is second only to the family relationship.

A young man who participates in a fifty-miler positions himself to grow as a priesthood holder. One of the great parts of each day on the trail is when we group together as a body of priesthood holders, being a long way into the wilderness, and very sincerely pray for a good and safe day each morning and humbly thank the Lord for watching over us each evening.

Once, on a fifty-miler in the Wind River Range of Wyoming, our group found itself at the bottom of a tall ridge. We needed to hike over it to get to our next campsite, but a severe storm was quickly heading right for the ridge—lots of lightning and thunder. We couldn't stay where we were, there would be too much distance to make up the next day. One of the quorum members suggested we pray. We did. We felt all right about going on, so we did our part and high-tailed it up the trail, despite how tired we felt. When we reached the top of the ridge, the storm was almost upon us. But just before it got to us, it stopped, then divided—most of it going south and a part of it going north of us. We made it to the campsite with barely a few drops of rain on us. It was a potent reminder of the power of prayer for that group of priesthood holders. Individual and tent prayers are always encouraged, but they came especially easy that night. Spiritual thoughts can be extra keenly felt deep in the woods, a long way from home.

Self-reliance is an important staple of each day, but service to a fellow group member may be necessary to help him face a challenging part of a day. On one particular hike, I saw an older boy quietly stow into his pack much more than his share of the tent so that his smaller friend and tent mate would have an easier go of making it up a significant climb that day. Young Aaronic Priesthood holders may also witness service firsthand in the form of priesthood blessings on such hikes. Such was the case when on one hike a young man's heels became so badly blistered before he notified anyone of his situation that there was hardly enough moleskin, gauze, and tape to treat him for the remaining days. We did the best we could, creating what we called "bionic heels," but he still had four days to go, and we all knew the pain would be intense. So, his father and another leader administered to him. The next day he was bounding about with the best of them. The results of that blessing did not go unnoticed by any of us, young or old.

It has been my experience that a fifty-miler can be a strong asset to the emotional and mental preparation one needs for a mission. Just going on a fifty-miler succeeds in this respect because, like a mission, it is daunting but significantly rewarding. When a young man completes a fifty-mile hike, he is more likely to view a mission as accomplishable, even though it will mean a lot of hard work, because he has glimpsed the reward and satisfaction that comes through overcoming. The whole idea that things of value take effort mentally, physically, and emotionally begins to materialize. A young man can see with greater understanding and confidence that he will complete his mission honorably because he has already done so on a smaller scale.

At the end of a particularly hard hike, one young man came into his home, dropped his pack in the middle of the living room, and said to his parents, "If I can do that, I can do anything." According to his parents, there was no bravado in his statement, but pure, sincere confidence. He went on to fulfill a good and honorable mission, the first and only one of his siblings to do so.

There is a wholesome pride attached to and a confidence gained from completing such a week-long event. In fact, there are but few experiences that can teach a person the principle of enduring to the end like the fifty-miler does. Completing such a trek underscores one's view that mortality has a beginning and an end with a lot of steps and stumbles in between. And the way we make it to the end is one step at a time, resolving each day to get up and make it to the close of day. Basically, a young man's vision of his ability to complete life more successfully clarifies and solidifies.

On the Sunday just before one fifty-miler, our quorum lesson was on enduring to the end, making it from point A to point B in life. We talked about the lives of great men who had made it from point A to point B, despite imposing difficulties. That week, we did the fifty-miler. The next

Sunday one young man raised his hand high, right at the beginning of class, and said, "Brother Harrison, *we* made it from point A to point B. We endured to the end." We could have ended the lesson right there. I've never smiled as big as I did when I turned to him and replied, "Yes. We did!"

Is a fifty-miler a panacea? No. But it is a tremendously valuable tool to help teach and prepare our young men to more successfully and faithfully live the life that lies before them. After all, the Lord has used extended "hikes" frequently to prepare and refine His people, especially before they were to inherit a promised land (the Jaredites, Nephites, children of Israel, and the Mormon pioneers). We as leaders can do the same, in miniature, to guide, prepare, and refine those we serve . . . via the fifty-miler.

Ode to a Fifty-miler*

We entered into one of the most spectacular but rugged and unforgiving wildernesses in North America. We stood face to face with the elements—storm, lightning, rain, hail, wind, incline, and insects—pressing forward day by day. We bowed our backs under our packs striving toward our goal, some struggling against spreading, bleeding blisters, others against sickness, most all against over-taxed sinew and muscle. We ascended three passes well over 10,000 feet and descended into granite gorges far below. We forded four rivers and countless streams until on the fifth day we emerged the wearied but certain conquerors—a fellowship of twelve having smiled and laughed even sung throughout, having grown stronger and closer, especially enjoying the Spirit along our route. And thus in brief went a great adventure, but one which, for this stouthearted corps, will assuredly but preface other adventures of equally great or greater dimension—whose own tales, in time, will yet be told.

(*A commendation given to those who completed one of the more difficult fifty-milers I've been on—completed in four and a half days along a difficult route in the Wind River Mountains of western Wyoming.)

9

Wilderness Object Lessons

Guideline: Use wilderness activities to serve as gospel object lessons.

Insight: Physical experiences or symbols augment our understanding of spiritual principles.

The Sweat Lodge

"Yeah."

"Dude."

"Oogh, oogh, oogh (gorilla victory grunts)."

Such were the responses to my announcement of the first-ever sweat lodge for my present troop of scouts. The sweat lodge sounded cool and manly. Of course, many things sound cool and manly to twelve- and thirteen-year-olds. But this really did: sitting in a sweat lodge at midnight in one's swimming suit, drinking pop, and waiting to see the white buffalo, and then, once the white buffalo has been seen, quickly exiting to jump into a nearby snow bank or creek. How cool can it get?

In case someone reading this is scratching his head, wondering what a sweat lodge is, here's a quick overview. For my scout sweat lodges, I use a simple structure of PVC pipes covered with several plastic tarps to imitate a small hut. I place eight to ten melon-sized hot rocks in a small clump in the center. Six to eight participants enter the lodge. I close the flap so that no drafts of outside air can come in, then begin sprinkling water from a bucket on the rocks. Steam fills the hut and all begin sweating—sweating a lot. After five to ten minutes, I declare that the white buffalo has been seen. I lift the flap and all head out to jump in the snow or wash in the creek. This quickly cleans off the sweat and closes up the pores. Everyone dries off, changes, and then joins together at the campfire. Afterward, most every-one with a proper bedroll sleeps like a baby.

After the troop meeting, despite a fairly detailed description of the sweat lodge experience, I'm sure that most of the boys each had his own peculiar image of what the experience would actually be like. That would explain why on that coldish early-spring Friday night, after we had fin-ished dinner and I had mentioned that it was time for our sweat lodge and that everyone was to go change into his swimsuit, a few of the boys who were bundled in their warm clothes around the campfire looked at me uncomprehendingly: *What? Change into just a swimming suit when it's cold outside?*

They lingered around the campfire after the rest had gone to change, a little reluctant to leave their comfort zone and shed their warm coats. They suggested that maybe they would just watch this time. I countered with encouragement and a reminder that we only did this once in a great while, and so this would probably be their only chance. The boys decided to go ahead and get ready, except for one young boy who looked up at me with unblinking, timorous eyes and said he didn't think he could do it. I reassured him that if he would change quickly and get into the hut right away, he'd have one of the most incredible experiences so far in his life. He was still disbelieving but convinced just enough that he went to his tent to change. I waited outside until he was ready, and then accompanied him to the sweat lodge.

Once inside, I reviewed with the boys and leaders a little of the history of the sweat lodge. This was a hot rock sweat lodge, a type commonly used among Native Americans and their ancestors for centuries; however, the sweat lodge concept had been around for thousands of years: the Romans and Greeks used it as did the Persians and just about all ancient peoples, especially their warriors. The boys liked hearing that warriors used it to relax after battles, but I let them know it was also used for medicinal and spiritual purposes as well.

By the time I had finished this brief commentary, things were nice and toasty inside our little sweat lodge. I then took a cup, dipped it in the water bucket, and poured a small amount of water on the rocks. A steam cloud instantly hissed and filled the room. I poured some more water on the rocks. The steam became thicker, hotter.

"Hey, I can't see anything," complained one scout.

"I need to get out and cool off," said another.

"Patience, my young grasshoppers," I said. "We've only been in here a minute. We'll need to stay in at least five more minutes before we're ready to see the white buffalo. You'll know the time is right when you're sweating from every pore and when blowing on your arm makes it burn."

I sprinkled more water on the rocks. Then more again. The steam enveloped all of us. The sweat began to bead up in large droplets over every inch of our exposed skin. I poured a little more water on the rocks.

"How we doin' guys?" I asked.

"I'm burnin' hot," one scout replied.

"Are you sweatin' yet?" I inquired.

"No duh," the scout responded. "I'm sweating everywhere. My eyeballs are sweating."

"Then we're getting close," I announced.

I kept sprinkling water on the rocks to maintain the steam and heat.

"So, let's do a progress check," I said. "Everyone, blow on your arm."

There was a quick moment of quiet puffs then a flurry of astonished "Ows."

"Well, it looks like we're just about ready," I said. "But before we get ready to head out, just out of curiosity, I'd like to ask a strange question. Can anyone here tell me what sweat is made out of?"

"Body water," commented a young scout.

"Lick your arm," I said. He swiped his tongue briefly across his forearm.

"Salt. Salty water," he replied and licked again.

Others tried licking their arms.

A voice in the steamy cloud said, "So, what's up with this? Why are we licking our arms?"

"Well, I thought you'd be interested to know that not only does sweat contain water and minerals, like salt, but it can also have toxins in it. In fact, in many cultures, people would use the sweat lodge to help them sweat out impurities and illnesses."

"Yuck," said one scout. "I'm not licking anymore."

"No need to," I replied. "But knowing that you are probably covered in sweaty toxins and impurities and knowing that you aren't feeling very comfortable in this steam, you might understand why we are going to do what we are going to do next. Just a minute ago most of you could think of nothing else but getting out of here to get cool and more comfortable. Now, you might want to clean off as well.

"In a minute, I'm going to open the flap. One by one, all of us are going to exit as quickly and safely as possible. Be careful not to touch the rocks—they're still a bit hot. Then cross over the twenty feet or so to the little creek nearby and get into it. Submerge yourself quickly in the water either by lying in it, if you can find a suitable place, or by splashing the water all over yourself so that all the sweat has been washed away. Think only about getting all the sweat off as fast as you can. Don't think about anything else. Just do it. Afterwards, dry off with your towel and go change."

I tilted my pop can over the rocks and let two small drops spill out onto the rocks. A pungent cream soda steam filled the hut.

"That smells," said one of the scouts.

"My eyes are burning," uttered another, cupping his hands over his eyes.

"Yep, and with that pungent aroma filling our nostrils, I declare that the White Buffalo has been seen."

I threw open the flap and said, "Let's go! Everybody in the water!"

A line of sweaty, hot bodies dashed to the creek. We'd hung a lantern to light the area. Despite the fact that the water was coming from the snow fields above, we all got in, even my timorous-eyed scout. Some lay down and rolled in the creek. Others knelt down and scooped and splashed, but all washed off. A few snowflakes began to fall in the cooling late night air. We hardly noticed. We still generated so much heat that as soon as a snow flake touched one of us it vanished. We got out of the water, dried off, and then stood with our towels around our necks, looking up into the night unaffected by the coolness even though we were outside in swimming trunks with light snow falling on us.

That warm euphoria didn't last forever, so after a bit we headed to our tents to change. After changing, we gathered around the newly resuscitated campfire for our closing songs, stories, treats, and a spiritual thought for the day. It was late, so we abbreviated everything, and when it came time for me to conclude with a few thoughts, I mentioned to the boys that tonight for my spiritual thought all I had was a solitary question: "Why does the sweat lodge experience remind us of baptism?"

Reviewing the numerous Sunday school lessons they'd been a part of, a few boys saw the similarities instantly. They commented that the uncomfortable heat and sweaty toxins were like sins and that the water washing them clean was like baptism. The others listened and reviewed the sweat lodge experience in light of the memory of their own not-too-distantly received baptisms. But based on the thoughtful stares on all of the boys' faces, what happened during their baptismal ordinance seemed to register more clearly. And to them, through that symbolic representation of baptism during the sweat lodge experience, the spiritual reality of what happened during their baptism became more comprehendible. The young men reflected quietly for a moment without encouragement. In that moment, the Spirit touched them, and though it technically needs no external help, I believe the Spirit enjoyed the scene that was set to help teach those young men about this doctrine of the gospel.

We closed with a kneeling prayer around the campfire and then headed to our beds. There was some subdued talking in the individual tents, but it didn't last long. Soon all were asleep in a state of uncommon relaxation, one enhanced by the sound of the nearby stream washing over the rocks and by a warm sense of comfort and wellness, which pampered all into the sound repose that only those who have recently seen the white buffalo can enjoy.

10

Quiet Time

Guideline: Use peaceful wilderness moments to teach about listening to the Spirit.

Insight: Be still to hear the still, small voice.

Conversations in the Wild

It was close to springtime and the mountains were still filled with snow. In fact, it had just snowed the day before, coating the trees with about two to three inches of new snow. The clouds had cleared from the storm, leaving a beautiful blue sky above. The morning temperature was crisp but not frigid. Today was Saturday and my son, Andrew, and I had planned a snowshoeing excursion with a small picnic lunch to check out a route we were later hoping to take others on. The day could not have been more beautiful.

We had planned to do a loop of several miles, stopping at the halfway point for lunch. From the trailhead, we followed a creek for about a mile until it forked, at which point we took the left fork up a draw between two heavily forested hills. The new snow was deep and soft. We were the first to leave any tracks in the newly whitened landscape. We felt like mountain men discovering new territory for the first time in human history. It also helped that there was no one else around, anywhere.

It was Andrew's first snowshoeing trip, so I volunteered to break trail. We both wore gaiters to keep the snow out of our boots and keep the lower part of our legs dry and warm. Our snowshoes were sinking about six inches each time we stepped into new snow. There was a soft wisp and crunch with each step as we made our way around the occasional brush and old-growth trees. After about another mile, we broke out into a little clearing where two drainages came together. We climbed up a small ridge nearby and stomped down a small area of snow so we could sit down and start lunch. As we got lunch ready, the sun came full over the mountains and radiated warmly on the clearing and forest around us.

We were anxious to eat, so we rustled roughly through our backpacks, pulling out our sandwiches, fruit, dessert, and stove and fuel for heating water for hot chocolate. Once we got the stove lit and the flame blaring beneath the pot of water, we leaned back on our packs and soaked up the sun while downing lunch, one large, quick bite after another. The water was just starting to boil when I turned off the stove, took the pot, and poured some hot water into our cups. With the noise of the pressured gas flame gone and most of our zealous chewing done, I turned to Andrew and said, "Boy, it's sure quiet here." Since his mouth was full, he cocked his head, slid his eyes from side to side, paused, raised his eyebrows, and nodded. We then dumped our hot chocolate packets into our cups and stirred. While waiting for the hot chocolate to cool, we shared a few comments about the terrain, the beauty of the forest, and the sunshine warming us. We took a tentative quick sip from our cups to test the hotness of our drinks, and then just sat there, gazing across the clearing out into the forest and up the sides of the nearby mountains. It was the kind of father-son moment where we didn't need to speak. We just sat together and enjoyed gazing, both content with the company and the surroundings.

Sitting there, sipping the hot chocolate, I could hear the birds and chipmunks up in the trees. It sounded like they were all conversing.

I said, "The chipmunks and birds are sure noisy today."

He nodded and looked up at the tree tops trying to spot some of them.

"But it's really quiet too," he said

I listened for a minute and said, "Yes, it is. Maybe the contrast of the quiet forest makes the chipmunk chatter more noticeable."

We listened some more. Then suddenly we got splatted by some small, wet snowballs from directly overhead.

"Where did that come from," I asked.

We looked above us for a moment when a couple of larger "snow bombs" hurtled down and blasted the snow nearby us.

"Hey. I think it's the sun melting the snow on the tree branches, and the snow is melting and falling off the trees," said Andrew.

"I think you're right. Let's move out of the line of fire."

We scooted ourselves and gear away from the trees.

After getting repositioned, we concentrated on watching the snow bombs fall from the trees around us. But in watching, we were equally enthralled at listening to the muffled, soft cannonade happening all around. We became very still so as to try and hear even the distant "bombings." The bombings became so frequent at one point that it was like the forest was doing its own version of an applause for the sun coming out, like lots of people clapping with mittens on. Then in the middle of this arrhythmic plopping, the sound of a large branch breaking startled us. It came from across the clearing. Then another branch broke in the same vicinity. Andrew and I looked at each other with a look that said, "Was that naturally caused or big-animal caused?"

I involuntarily leaned forward and squinted, as though that would sharpen my hearing. I suppressed my breathing as much as possible, almost trying to stop my heart so that not even a heartbeat would interfere with my concentrated stillness. I listened for some patternlike crunching of the snow, some brushing of a bush. Nothing. That was actually a good thing. No such sounds meant that there was probably no moody moose or half-starved bear out of early hibernation coming for us. But to make sure, I listened again, my adrenaline making each ear strain to be twice as big as normal.

For the next minute, a statue might have moved more than I did. And poised so, Andrew and I began to hear sounds we hadn't heard before. We heard many branches breaking—some faintly, a long ways away. We heard snow slipping off of branches, landing on other branches. We could distinguish the whoosh of needles whipping through the air as a branch would spring back into place after the snow left it. We heard bird calls but now noticed the difference between the calls of one bird versus another. From far up a nearby canyon, we heard a low rumbling that gradually faded, and we suspected we had just heard an avalanche since there was not a cloud in the sky. The wilderness had been quiet to our casual listening before, but with our intense stillness we now heard a multitude of wilderness comments. In fact, we were right in the middle of wilderness conversations of manifold proportion, though still and soft in their delivery.

Andrew and I sat and listened for a while longer and then leaned back and shook our heads as though we had received a surfeit of information and could no longer process any more.

I smiled and said to Andrew, "Well . . . I think it's time to head back, but this has been incredible." Andrew looked over and agreed. We put our things back into the packs and swung them onto our backs. As we stood up and began to move off, we took another look around our special spot hoping not to let the memory of our experience there dissipate. Then we moved off into the trees and headed back to the trailhead.

The memory of that experience has not dissipated. When I recall it, I think of how much there was to hear when we lent an ear and focused on that special opportunity. I remember how still we had to be to hear and learn from those wilderness comments. I think of how truly taught we were. And I am grateful for that experience because it has become a reference point for what it takes to hear and learn from the still, small voice of the Spirit. Thanks to that wilderness experience, I have a greater insight into what the Lord means when He says, "Be still, and know that I am God"—I believe He's expecting me to lean forward and ready myself for his version of a conversation in the wild.

Conclusion

You know that you've arrived when . . .

You know that you have arrived . . . when you're there. That's how I think the adaptable idiomatic expression reads in its ultimate form, but along the way, we may experience preparatory versions of this like: "You know you've arrived when you have fewer blisters than toes" or "You know you've arrived when getting there is as much fun as being there." The basic idea is that there is a journey and a destination. When the destination is a long way off, then the journey takes on added significance. Since most of us want to end up with an address somewhere high in the clouds, we can assume that our journey will be an upward one. And with that in mind, to make the journey more doable, the secret is to learn to prefer the up. Now, that's easier said than done. But a few notable persons have "arrived" in that respect.

One such person was a prominent religious figure I once heard speak. In that particular address, he said that he welcomed trials. When I heard that, all I could do was grimace in uncomprehending disbelief. Why would anyone welcome more of that which most of us pray to avoid? I don't know that I can ever comprehend how the speaker was able to say that, but somehow along the way he had come to an understanding that to welcome trials hastened and embellished his journey to his ultimate goal or destination. And to him, that was more desirable than trying to take the easy way. On his trail map, he truly saw downhill as the great deceit. Along the way he had answered the question posed in Psalm 24:3: "Who shall ascend into the hill of the Lord?"

For this person, the answer was, "He who is willing to ascend." So, he and those who have reached this echelon in life have learned to prefer the up, maybe not in the sense of having fun while ascending, although I wouldn't put it out of the reach of some, but preferring it to the alternative.

For me, though I cannot claim to be on the same plain with such people, I have glimpsed with improved understanding how they could ultimately prefer the up, and it has been the wilderness that has helped teach me this. Each time I put on my hiking boots and head up and away from the frenzy of day-to-day living, I am reminded that going up will get me to places where I enjoy greater perspective and purity, places that bring me joy in being there. I can look about and think that despite the up, I am glad I'm here. It has been the meaningful lessons on the mountain that have instilled in me an appreciation for going up and for where going up ultimately takes me. And someday, I hope to relate to those who truly comprehend and prefer the up, for then I will know that I have arrived.

About the Author

Mark Harrison grew up in the Pacific Northwest where he learned to love the wilderness from hiking and camping in the Cascade Mountains. He has climbed Mt. Rainier and hiked in most of the great mountain ranges of the western United States and Canada. He has been on over two hundred campouts and deep wilderness adventures with Boy Scouts, youth groups, and family.

He presently lives in American Fork, Utah, with his wife, Debbie. They are the parents of six children. He has served as a bishop, high councilor, and scoutmaster. He seeks every chance he can to go mountain biking, hiking, camping, or snowshoeing. After God and family, he finds his greatest strength from being in the great out-of-doors.